WHAT ANTIFA ENGAGES IN

E.J. RAEB

ISBN 13: 9781720267584

Blank Page

Violence
Suppressing Free Speech
Riots
Anarchy
Suppressing Opinion
Fascism

Violence
Suppressing Free Speech
Riots
Anarchy
Suppressing Opinion
Fascism

Violence
Suppressing Free Speech
Riots
Anarchy
Suppressing Opinion
Fascism

Violence
Suppressing Free Speech
Riots
Anarchy
Suppressing Opinion
Fascism

Violence
Suppressing Free Speech
Riots
Anarchy
Suppressing Opinion
Fascism

Violence
Suppressing Free Speech
Riots
Anarchy
Suppressing Opinion
Fascism

Violence
Suppressing Free Speech
Riots
Anarchy
Suppressing Opinion
Fascism

Violence
Suppressing Free Speech
Riots
Anarchy
Suppressing Opinion
Fascism

Violence
Suppressing Free Speech
Riots
Anarchy
Suppressing Opinion
Fascism

Violence
Suppressing Free Speech
Riots
Anarchy
Suppressing Opinion
Fascism

Violence
Suppressing Free Speech
Riots
Anarchy
Suppressing Opinion
Fascism

Violence
Suppressing Free Speech
Riots
Anarchy
Suppressing Opinion
Fascism

Violence

Suppressing Free Speech

Riots

Anarchy

Suppressing Opinion

Fascism

Violence

Suppressing Free Speech

Riots

Anarchy

Suppressing Opinion

Fascism

Violence

Suppressing Free Speech

Riots

Anarchy

Suppressing Opinion

Fascism

Violence
Suppressing Free Speech
Riots
Anarchy
Suppressing Opinion
Fascism

Violence
Suppressing Free Speech
Riots
Anarchy
Suppressing Opinion
Fascism

Violence
Suppressing Free Speech
Riots
Anarchy
Suppressing Opinion
Fascism

Violence
Suppressing Free Speech
Riots
Anarchy
Suppressing Opinion
Fascism

Violence
Suppressing Free Speech
Riots
Anarchy
Suppressing Opinion
Fascism

Violence
Suppressing Free Speech
Riots
Anarchy
Suppressing Opinion
Fascism

Violence
Suppressing Free Speech
Riots
Anarchy
Suppressing Opinion
Fascism

Violence
Suppressing Free Speech
Riots
Anarchy
Suppressing Opinion
Fascism

Violence
Suppressing Free Speech
Riots
Anarchy
Suppressing Opinion
Fascism

Violence
Suppressing Free Speech
Riots
Anarchy
Suppressing Opinion
Fascism

Violence
Suppressing Free Speech
Riots
Anarchy
Suppressing Opinion
Fascism

Violence
Suppressing Free Speech
Riots
Anarchy
Suppressing Opinion
Fascism

Violence
Suppressing Free Speech
Riots
Anarchy
Suppressing Opinion
Fascism

Violence
Suppressing Free Speech
Riots
Anarchy
Suppressing Opinion
Fascism

Violence
Suppressing Free Speech
Riots
Anarchy
Suppressing Opinion
Fascism

Violence
Suppressing Free Speech
Riots
Anarchy
Suppressing Opinion
Fascism

Violence
Suppressing Free Speech
Riots
Anarchy
Suppressing Opinion
Fascism

Violence
Suppressing Free Speech
Riots
Anarchy
Suppressing Opinion
Fascism

Violence
Suppressing Free Speech
Riots
Anarchy
Suppressing Opinion
Fascism

Violence
Suppressing Free Speech
Riots
Anarchy
Suppressing Opinion
Fascism

Violence
Suppressing Free Speech
Riots
Anarchy
Suppressing Opinion
Fascism

Violence
Suppressing Free Speech
Riots
Anarchy
Suppressing Opinion
Fascism

Violence
Suppressing Free Speech
Riots
Anarchy
Suppressing Opinion
Fascism

Violence
Suppressing Free Speech
Riots
Anarchy
Suppressing Opinion
Fascism

Violence
Suppressing Free Speech
Riots
Anarchy
Suppressing Opinion
Fascism

Violence
Suppressing Free Speech
Riots
Anarchy
Suppressing Opinion
Fascism

Violence
Suppressing Free Speech
Riots
Anarchy
Suppressing Opinion
Fascism

Violence
Suppressing Free Speech
Riots
Anarchy
Suppressing Opinion
Fascism

Violence
Suppressing Free Speech
Riots
Anarchy
Suppressing Opinion
Fascism

Violence
Suppressing Free Speech
Riots
Anarchy
Suppressing Opinion
Fascism

Violence
Suppressing Free Speech
Riots
Anarchy
Suppressing Opinion
Fascism

Violence
Suppressing Free Speech
Riots
Anarchy
Suppressing Opinion
Fascism

Violence
Suppressing Free Speech
Riots
Anarchy
Suppressing Opinion
Fascism

Violence
Suppressing Free Speech
Riots
Anarchy
Suppressing Opinion
Fascism

Violence
Suppressing Free Speech
Riots
Anarchy
Suppressing Opinion
Fascism

Violence
Suppressing Free Speech
Riots
Anarchy
Suppressing Opinion
Fascism

Violence
Suppressing Free Speech
Riots
Anarchy
Suppressing Opinion
Fascism

Violence
Suppressing Free Speech
Riots
Anarchy
Suppressing Opinion
Fascism

Violence
Suppressing Free Speech
Riots
Anarchy
Suppressing Opinion
Fascism

Violence
Suppressing Free Speech
Riots
Anarchy
Suppressing Opinion
Fascism

Violence
Suppressing Free Speech
Riots
Anarchy
Suppressing Opinion
Fascism

Violence
Suppressing Free Speech
Riots
Anarchy
Suppressing Opinion
Fascism

Violence
Suppressing Free Speech
Riots
Anarchy
Suppressing Opinion
Fascism

Violence
Suppressing Free Speech
Riots
Anarchy
Suppressing Opinion
Fascism

Violence
Suppressing Free Speech
Riots
Anarchy
Suppressing Opinion
Fascism

Violence
Suppressing Free Speech
Riots
Anarchy
Suppressing Opinion
Fascism

Violence
Suppressing Free Speech
Riots
Anarchy
Suppressing Opinion
Fascism

Violence
Suppressing Free Speech
Riots
Anarchy
Suppressing Opinion
Fascism

Violence
Suppressing Free Speech
Riots
Anarchy
Suppressing Opinion
Fascism

Violence
Suppressing Free Speech
Riots
Anarchy
Suppressing Opinion
Fascism

Violence
Suppressing Free Speech
Riots
Anarchy
Suppressing Opinion
Fascism

Violence
Suppressing Free Speech
Riots
Anarchy
Suppressing Opinion
Fascism

Violence
Suppressing Free Speech
Riots
Anarchy
Suppressing Opinion
Fascism

Violence
Suppressing Free Speech
Riots
Anarchy
Suppressing Opinion
Fascism

Violence
Suppressing Free Speech
Riots
Anarchy
Suppressing Opinion
Fascism

Violence
Suppressing Free Speech
Riots
Anarchy
Suppressing Opinion
Fascism

Violence
Suppressing Free Speech
Riots
Anarchy
Suppressing Opinion
Fascism

Violence
Suppressing Free Speech
Riots
Anarchy
Suppressing Opinion
Fascism

Violence
Suppressing Free Speech
Riots
Anarchy
Suppressing Opinion
Fascism

Violence
Suppressing Free Speech
Riots
Anarchy
Suppressing Opinion
Fascism

Violence
Suppressing Free Speech
Riots
Anarchy
Suppressing Opinion
Fascism

Violence
Suppressing Free Speech
Riots
Anarchy
Suppressing Opinion
Fascism

Violence
Suppressing Free Speech
Riots
Anarchy
Suppressing Opinion
Fascism

Violence
Suppressing Free Speech
Riots
Anarchy
Suppressing Opinion
Fascism

Violence
Suppressing Free Speech
Riots
Anarchy
Suppressing Opinion
Fascism

Violence
Suppressing Free Speech
Riots
Anarchy
Suppressing Opinion
Fascism

Violence
Suppressing Free Speech
Riots
Anarchy
Suppressing Opinion
Fascism

Violence
Suppressing Free Speech
Riots
Anarchy
Suppressing Opinion
Fascism

Violence
Suppressing Free Speech
Riots
Anarchy
Suppressing Opinion
Fascism

Violence
Suppressing Free Speech
Riots
Anarchy
Suppressing Opinion
Fascism

Violence
Suppressing Free Speech
Riots
Anarchy
Suppressing Opinion
Fascism

Violence
Suppressing Free Speech
Riots
Anarchy
Suppressing Opinion
Fascism

Violence
Suppressing Free Speech
Riots
Anarchy
Suppressing Opinion
Fascism

Violence
Suppressing Free Speech
Riots
Anarchy
Suppressing Opinion
Fascism

Violence
Suppressing Free Speech
Riots
Anarchy
Suppressing Opinion
Fascism

Violence
Suppressing Free Speech
Riots
Anarchy
Suppressing Opinion
Fascism

Violence
Suppressing Free Speech
Riots
Anarchy
Suppressing Opinion
Fascism

Violence
Suppressing Free Speech
Riots
Anarchy
Suppressing Opinion
Fascism

Violence
Suppressing Free Speech
Riots
Anarchy
Suppressing Opinion
Fascism

Violence
Suppressing Free Speech
Riots
Anarchy
Suppressing Opinion
Fascism

Violence
Suppressing Free Speech
Riots
Anarchy
Suppressing Opinion
Fascism

Violence
Suppressing Free Speech
Riots
Anarchy
Suppressing Opinion
Fascism

Violence
Suppressing Free Speech
Riots
Anarchy
Suppressing Opinion
Fascism

Violence
Suppressing Free Speech
Riots
Anarchy
Suppressing Opinion
Fascism

Violence
Suppressing Free Speech
Riots
Anarchy
Suppressing Opinion
Fascism

Violence
Suppressing Free Speech
Riots
Anarchy
Suppressing Opinion
Fascism

Violence
Suppressing Free Speech
Riots
Anarchy
Suppressing Opinion
Fascism

Violence
Suppressing Free Speech
Riots
Anarchy
Suppressing Opinion
Fascism

Violence
Suppressing Free Speech
Riots
Anarchy
Suppressing Opinion
Fascism

Violence
Suppressing Free Speech
Riots
Anarchy
Suppressing Opinion
Fascism

Violence
Suppressing Free Speech
Riots
Anarchy
Suppressing Opinion
Fascism

Violence
Suppressing Free Speech
Riots
Anarchy
Suppressing Opinion
Fascism

Violence
Suppressing Free Speech
Riots
Anarchy
Suppressing Opinion
Fascism

Violence
Suppressing Free Speech
Riots
Anarchy
Suppressing Opinion
Fascism

Violence
Suppressing Free Speech
Riots
Anarchy
Suppressing Opinion
Fascism

Violence
Suppressing Free Speech
Riots
Anarchy
Suppressing Opinion
Fascism

Violence
Suppressing Free Speech
Riots
Anarchy
Suppressing Opinion
Fascism

Violence
Suppressing Free Speech
Riots
Anarchy
Suppressing Opinion
Fascism

Violence
Suppressing Free Speech
Riots
Anarchy
Suppressing Opinion
Fascism

Violence
Suppressing Free Speech
Riots
Anarchy
Suppressing Opinion
Fascism

Violence
Suppressing Free Speech
Riots
Anarchy
Suppressing Opinion
Fascism

Violence
Suppressing Free Speech
Riots
Anarchy
Suppressing Opinion
Fascism

Violence
Suppressing Free Speech
Riots
Anarchy
Suppressing Opinion
Fascism

Violence
Suppressing Free Speech
Riots
Anarchy
Suppressing Opinion
Fascism

Violence
Suppressing Free Speech
Riots
Anarchy
Suppressing Opinion
Fascism

Violence
Suppressing Free Speech
Riots
Anarchy
Suppressing Opinion
Fascism

Violence
Suppressing Free Speech
Riots
Anarchy
Suppressing Opinion
Fascism

Violence
Suppressing Free Speech
Riots
Anarchy
Suppressing Opinion
Fascism

Violence
Suppressing Free Speech
Riots
Anarchy
Suppressing Opinion
Fascism

Violence
Suppressing Free Speech
Riots
Anarchy
Suppressing Opinion
Fascism

Violence
Suppressing Free Speech
Riots
Anarchy
Suppressing Opinion
Fascism

Violence
Suppressing Free Speech
Riots
Anarchy
Suppressing Opinion
Fascism

Violence
Suppressing Free Speech
Riots
Anarchy
Suppressing Opinion
Fascism

Violence
Suppressing Free Speech
Riots
Anarchy
Suppressing Opinion
Fascism

Violence
Suppressing Free Speech
Riots
Anarchy
Suppressing Opinion
Fascism

Violence
Suppressing Free Speech
Riots
Anarchy
Suppressing Opinion
Fascism

Violence
Suppressing Free Speech
Riots
Anarchy
Suppressing Opinion
Fascism

Violence
Suppressing Free Speech
Riots
Anarchy
Suppressing Opinion
Fascism

Violence
Suppressing Free Speech
Riots
Anarchy
Suppressing Opinion
Fascism

Violence
Suppressing Free Speech
Riots
Anarchy
Suppressing Opinion
Fascism

Violence
Suppressing Free Speech
Riots
Anarchy
Suppressing Opinion
Fascism

Violence
Suppressing Free Speech
Riots
Anarchy
Suppressing Opinion
Fascism

Violence
Suppressing Free Speech
Riots
Anarchy
Suppressing Opinion
Fascism

Violence
Suppressing Free Speech
Riots
Anarchy
Suppressing Opinion
Fascism

Violence
Suppressing Free Speech
Riots
Anarchy
Suppressing Opinion
Fascism

Violence
Suppressing Free Speech
Riots
Anarchy
Suppressing Opinion
Fascism

Violence
Suppressing Free Speech
Riots
Anarchy
Suppressing Opinion
Fascism

Violence
Suppressing Free Speech
Riots
Anarchy
Suppressing Opinion
Fascism

Violence
Suppressing Free Speech
Riots
Anarchy
Suppressing Opinion
Fascism

Violence
Suppressing Free Speech
Riots
Anarchy
Suppressing Opinion
Fascism

Violence
Suppressing Free Speech
Riots
Anarchy
Suppressing Opinion
Fascism

Violence
Suppressing Free Speech
Riots
Anarchy
Suppressing Opinion
Fascism

Violence
Suppressing Free Speech
Riots
Anarchy
Suppressing Opinion
Fascism

Violence
Suppressing Free Speech
Riots
Anarchy
Suppressing Opinion
Fascism

Violence
Suppressing Free Speech
Riots
Anarchy
Suppressing Opinion
Fascism

Violence
Suppressing Free Speech
Riots
Anarchy
Suppressing Opinion
Fascism

Violence
Suppressing Free Speech
Riots
Anarchy
Suppressing Opinion
Fascism

Violence
Suppressing Free Speech
Riots
Anarchy
Suppressing Opinion
Fascism

Violence
Suppressing Free Speech
Riots
Anarchy
Suppressing Opinion
Fascism

Violence
Suppressing Free Speech
Riots
Anarchy
Suppressing Opinion
Fascism

Violence
Suppressing Free Speech
Riots
Anarchy
Suppressing Opinion
Fascism

Violence
Suppressing Free Speech
Riots
Anarchy
Suppressing Opinion
Fascism

Violence
Suppressing Free Speech
Riots
Anarchy
Suppressing Opinion
Fascism

Violence
Suppressing Free Speech
Riots
Anarchy
Suppressing Opinion
Fascism

Violence
Suppressing Free Speech
Riots
Anarchy
Suppressing Opinion
Fascism

Violence
Suppressing Free Speech
Riots
Anarchy
Suppressing Opinion
Fascism

Violence
Suppressing Free Speech
Riots
Anarchy
Suppressing Opinion
Fascism

Violence
Suppressing Free Speech
Riots
Anarchy
Suppressing Opinion
Fascism

Violence
Suppressing Free Speech
Riots
Anarchy
Suppressing Opinion
Fascism

Violence
Suppressing Free Speech
Riots
Anarchy
Suppressing Opinion
Fascism

Violence
Suppressing Free Speech
Riots
Anarchy
Suppressing Opinion
Fascism

Violence
Suppressing Free Speech
Riots
Anarchy
Suppressing Opinion
Fascism

Violence
Suppressing Free Speech
Riots
Anarchy
Suppressing Opinion
Fascism

Violence
Suppressing Free Speech
Riots
Anarchy
Suppressing Opinion
Fascism

Violence
Suppressing Free Speech
Riots
Anarchy
Suppressing Opinion
Fascism

Violence
Suppressing Free Speech
Riots
Anarchy
Suppressing Opinion
Fascism

Violence
Suppressing Free Speech
Riots
Anarchy
Suppressing Opinion
Fascism

Violence
Suppressing Free Speech
Riots
Anarchy
Suppressing Opinion
Fascism

Violence
Suppressing Free Speech
Riots
Anarchy
Suppressing Opinion
Fascism

Violence
Suppressing Free Speech
Riots
Anarchy
Suppressing Opinion
Fascism

Violence
Suppressing Free Speech
Riots
Anarchy
Suppressing Opinion
Fascism

Violence
Suppressing Free Speech
Riots
Anarchy
Suppressing Opinion
Fascism

Violence
Suppressing Free Speech
Riots
Anarchy
Suppressing Opinion
Fascism

Violence
Suppressing Free Speech
Riots
Anarchy
Suppressing Opinion
Fascism

Violence
Suppressing Free Speech
Riots
Anarchy
Suppressing Opinion
Fascism

Violence
Suppressing Free Speech
Riots
Anarchy
Suppressing Opinion
Fascism

Violence
Suppressing Free Speech
Riots
Anarchy
Suppressing Opinion
Fascism

Violence
Suppressing Free Speech
Riots
Anarchy
Suppressing Opinion
Fascism

Violence
Suppressing Free Speech
Riots
Anarchy
Suppressing Opinion
Fascism

Violence
Suppressing Free Speech
Riots
Anarchy
Suppressing Opinion
Fascism

Violence
Suppressing Free Speech
Riots
Anarchy
Suppressing Opinion
Fascism

Violence
Suppressing Free Speech
Riots
Anarchy
Suppressing Opinion
Fascism

Violence
Suppressing Free Speech
Riots
Anarchy
Suppressing Opinion
Fascism

Violence
Suppressing Free Speech
Riots
Anarchy
Suppressing Opinion
Fascism

Violence
Suppressing Free Speech
Riots
Anarchy
Suppressing Opinion
Fascism

Violence
Suppressing Free Speech
Riots
Anarchy
Suppressing Opinion
Fascism

Violence
Suppressing Free Speech
Riots
Anarchy
Suppressing Opinion
Fascism

Violence
Suppressing Free Speech
Riots
Anarchy
Suppressing Opinion
Fascism

Violence
Suppressing Free Speech
Riots
Anarchy
Suppressing Opinion
Fascism

Violence
Suppressing Free Speech
Riots
Anarchy
Suppressing Opinion
Fascism

Violence
Suppressing Free Speech
Riots
Anarchy
Suppressing Opinion
Fascism

Violence
Suppressing Free Speech
Riots
Anarchy
Suppressing Opinion
Fascism

Violence
Suppressing Free Speech
Riots
Anarchy
Suppressing Opinion
Fascism

Violence
Suppressing Free Speech
Riots
Anarchy
Suppressing Opinion
Fascism

Violence
Suppressing Free Speech
Riots
Anarchy
Suppressing Opinion
Fascism

Violence
Suppressing Free Speech
Riots
Anarchy
Suppressing Opinion
Fascism

Violence
Suppressing Free Speech
Riots
Anarchy
Suppressing Opinion
Fascism

Violence
Suppressing Free Speech
Riots
Anarchy
Suppressing Opinion
Fascism

Violence
Suppressing Free Speech
Riots
Anarchy
Suppressing Opinion
Fascism

Violence
Suppressing Free Speech
Riots
Anarchy
Suppressing Opinion
Fascism

Violence
Suppressing Free Speech
Riots
Anarchy
Suppressing Opinion
Fascism

Violence
Suppressing Free Speech
Riots
Anarchy
Suppressing Opinion
Fascism

Violence
Suppressing Free Speech
Riots
Anarchy
Suppressing Opinion
Fascism

Violence
Suppressing Free Speech
Riots
Anarchy
Suppressing Opinion
Fascism

Violence
Suppressing Free Speech
Riots
Anarchy
Suppressing Opinion
Fascism

Violence
Suppressing Free Speech
Riots
Anarchy
Suppressing Opinion
Fascism

Violence
Suppressing Free Speech
Riots
Anarchy
Suppressing Opinion
Fascism

Violence
Suppressing Free Speech
Riots
Anarchy
Suppressing Opinion
Fascism

Violence
Suppressing Free Speech
Riots
Anarchy
Suppressing Opinion
Fascism

Violence
Suppressing Free Speech
Riots
Anarchy
Suppressing Opinion
Fascism

Violence
Suppressing Free Speech
Riots
Anarchy
Suppressing Opinion
Fascism

Violence
Suppressing Free Speech
Riots
Anarchy
Suppressing Opinion
Fascism

Violence
Suppressing Free Speech
Riots
Anarchy
Suppressing Opinion
Fascism

Violence
Suppressing Free Speech
Riots
Anarchy
Suppressing Opinion
Fascism

Violence
Suppressing Free Speech
Riots
Anarchy
Suppressing Opinion
Fascism

Violence
Suppressing Free Speech
Riots
Anarchy
Suppressing Opinion
Fascism

Violence
Suppressing Free Speech
Riots
Anarchy
Suppressing Opinion
Fascism

Violence
Suppressing Free Speech
Riots
Anarchy
Suppressing Opinion
Fascism

Violence
Suppressing Free Speech
Riots
Anarchy
Suppressing Opinion
Fascism

Violence
Suppressing Free Speech
Riots
Anarchy
Suppressing Opinion
Fascism

Violence
Suppressing Free Speech
Riots
Anarchy
Suppressing Opinion
Fascism

Violence
Suppressing Free Speech
Riots
Anarchy
Suppressing Opinion
Fascism

Violence
Suppressing Free Speech
Riots
Anarchy
Suppressing Opinion
Fascism

Violence
Suppressing Free Speech
Riots
Anarchy
Suppressing Opinion
Fascism

Violence
Suppressing Free Speech
Riots
Anarchy
Suppressing Opinion
Fascism

Violence
Suppressing Free Speech
Riots
Anarchy
Suppressing Opinion
Fascism

Violence
Suppressing Free Speech
Riots
Anarchy
Suppressing Opinion
Fascism

Violence
Suppressing Free Speech
Riots
Anarchy
Suppressing Opinion
Fascism

Violence
Suppressing Free Speech
Riots
Anarchy
Suppressing Opinion
Fascism

Violence
Suppressing Free Speech
Riots
Anarchy
Suppressing Opinion
Fascism

Violence
Suppressing Free Speech
Riots
Anarchy
Suppressing Opinion
Fascism

Violence
Suppressing Free Speech
Riots
Anarchy
Suppressing Opinion
Fascism

Violence
Suppressing Free Speech
Riots
Anarchy
Suppressing Opinion
Fascism

Violence
Suppressing Free Speech
Riots
Anarchy
Suppressing Opinion
Fascism

Violence
Suppressing Free Speech
Riots
Anarchy
Suppressing Opinion
Fascism

Violence
Suppressing Free Speech
Riots
Anarchy
Suppressing Opinion
Fascism

Violence
Suppressing Free Speech
Riots
Anarchy
Suppressing Opinion
Fascism

Violence
Suppressing Free Speech
Riots
Anarchy
Suppressing Opinion
Fascism

Violence
Suppressing Free Speech
Riots
Anarchy
Suppressing Opinion
Fascism

Violence
Suppressing Free Speech
Riots
Anarchy
Suppressing Opinion
Fascism

Violence
Suppressing Free Speech
Riots
Anarchy
Suppressing Opinion
Fascism

Violence
Suppressing Free Speech
Riots
Anarchy
Suppressing Opinion
Fascism

Violence
Suppressing Free Speech
Riots
Anarchy
Suppressing Opinion
Fascism

Violence
Suppressing Free Speech
Riots
Anarchy
Suppressing Opinion
Fascism

Violence
Suppressing Free Speech
Riots
Anarchy
Suppressing Opinion
Fascism

Violence
Suppressing Free Speech
Riots
Anarchy
Suppressing Opinion
Fascism

Violence
Suppressing Free Speech
Riots
Anarchy
Suppressing Opinion
Fascism

Violence
Suppressing Free Speech
Riots
Anarchy
Suppressing Opinion
Fascism

Violence
Suppressing Free Speech
Riots
Anarchy
Suppressing Opinion
Fascism

Violence
Suppressing Free Speech
Riots
Anarchy
Suppressing Opinion
Fascism

Violence
Suppressing Free Speech
Riots
Anarchy
Suppressing Opinion
Fascism

Violence
Suppressing Free Speech
Riots
Anarchy
Suppressing Opinion
Fascism

Violence
Suppressing Free Speech
Riots
Anarchy
Suppressing Opinion
Fascism

Violence
Suppressing Free Speech
Riots
Anarchy
Suppressing Opinion
Fascism

Violence
Suppressing Free Speech
Riots
Anarchy
Suppressing Opinion
Fascism

Violence
Suppressing Free Speech
Riots
Anarchy
Suppressing Opinion
Fascism

Violence
Suppressing Free Speech
Riots
Anarchy
Suppressing Opinion
Fascism

Violence
Suppressing Free Speech
Riots
Anarchy
Suppressing Opinion
Fascism

Violence
Suppressing Free Speech
Riots
Anarchy
Suppressing Opinion
Fascism

Violence
Suppressing Free Speech
Riots
Anarchy
Suppressing Opinion
Fascism

Violence
Suppressing Free Speech
Riots
Anarchy
Suppressing Opinion
Fascism

Violence
Suppressing Free Speech
Riots
Anarchy
Suppressing Opinion
Fascism

Violence
Suppressing Free Speech
Riots
Anarchy
Suppressing Opinion
Fascism

Violence
Suppressing Free Speech
Riots
Anarchy
Suppressing Opinion
Fascism

Violence
Suppressing Free Speech
Riots
Anarchy
Suppressing Opinion
Fascism

Violence
Suppressing Free Speech
Riots
Anarchy
Suppressing Opinion
Fascism

Violence
Suppressing Free Speech
Riots
Anarchy
Suppressing Opinion
Fascism

Violence
Suppressing Free Speech
Riots
Anarchy
Suppressing Opinion
Fascism

Violence
Suppressing Free Speech
Riots
Anarchy
Suppressing Opinion
Fascism

Violence
Suppressing Free Speech
Riots
Anarchy
Suppressing Opinion
Fascism

Violence
Suppressing Free Speech
Riots
Anarchy
Suppressing Opinion
Fascism

Violence
Suppressing Free Speech
Riots
Anarchy
Suppressing Opinion
Fascism

Violence
Suppressing Free Speech
Riots
Anarchy
Suppressing Opinion
Fascism

Violence
Suppressing Free Speech
Riots
Anarchy
Suppressing Opinion
Fascism

Violence
Suppressing Free Speech
Riots
Anarchy
Suppressing Opinion
Fascism

Violence
Suppressing Free Speech
Riots
Anarchy
Suppressing Opinion
Fascism

Violence
Suppressing Free Speech
Riots
Anarchy
Suppressing Opinion
Fascism

Violence
Suppressing Free Speech
Riots
Anarchy
Suppressing Opinion
Fascism

Violence
Suppressing Free Speech
Riots
Anarchy
Suppressing Opinion
Fascism

Violence
Suppressing Free Speech
Riots
Anarchy
Suppressing Opinion
Fascism

Violence
Suppressing Free Speech
Riots
Anarchy
Suppressing Opinion
Fascism

Violence
Suppressing Free Speech
Riots
Anarchy
Suppressing Opinion
Fascism

Violence
Suppressing Free Speech
Riots
Anarchy
Suppressing Opinion
Fascism

Violence
Suppressing Free Speech
Riots
Anarchy
Suppressing Opinion
Fascism

Violence
Suppressing Free Speech
Riots
Anarchy
Suppressing Opinion
Fascism

Violence
Suppressing Free Speech
Riots
Anarchy
Suppressing Opinion
Fascism

Violence
Suppressing Free Speech
Riots
Anarchy
Suppressing Opinion
Fascism

Violence
Suppressing Free Speech
Riots
Anarchy
Suppressing Opinion
Fascism

Violence
Suppressing Free Speech
Riots
Anarchy
Suppressing Opinion
Fascism

Violence
Suppressing Free Speech
Riots
Anarchy
Suppressing Opinion
Fascism

Violence
Suppressing Free Speech
Riots
Anarchy
Suppressing Opinion
Fascism

Violence
Suppressing Free Speech
Riots
Anarchy
Suppressing Opinion
Fascism

Violence
Suppressing Free Speech
Riots
Anarchy
Suppressing Opinion
Fascism

Violence
Suppressing Free Speech
Riots
Anarchy
Suppressing Opinion
Fascism

Violence
Suppressing Free Speech
Riots
Anarchy
Suppressing Opinion
Fascism

Violence
Suppressing Free Speech
Riots
Anarchy
Suppressing Opinion
Fascism

Violence
Suppressing Free Speech
Riots
Anarchy
Suppressing Opinion
Fascism

Violence
Suppressing Free Speech
Riots
Anarchy
Suppressing Opinion
Fascism

Violence
Suppressing Free Speech
Riots
Anarchy
Suppressing Opinion
Fascism

Violence
Suppressing Free Speech
Riots
Anarchy
Suppressing Opinion
Fascism

Violence
Suppressing Free Speech
Riots
Anarchy
Suppressing Opinion
Fascism

Violence
Suppressing Free Speech
Riots
Anarchy
Suppressing Opinion
Fascism

Violence
Suppressing Free Speech
Riots
Anarchy
Suppressing Opinion
Fascism

Violence
Suppressing Free Speech
Riots
Anarchy
Suppressing Opinion
Fascism

Violence
Suppressing Free Speech
Riots
Anarchy
Suppressing Opinion
Fascism

Violence
Suppressing Free Speech
Riots
Anarchy
Suppressing Opinion
Fascism

Violence
Suppressing Free Speech
Riots
Anarchy
Suppressing Opinion
Fascism

Violence
Suppressing Free Speech
Riots
Anarchy
Suppressing Opinion
Fascism

Violence
Suppressing Free Speech
Riots
Anarchy
Suppressing Opinion
Fascism

Violence
Suppressing Free Speech
Riots
Anarchy
Suppressing Opinion
Fascism

Violence
Suppressing Free Speech
Riots
Anarchy
Suppressing Opinion
Fascism

Violence
Suppressing Free Speech
Riots
Anarchy
Suppressing Opinion
Fascism

Violence
Suppressing Free Speech
Riots
Anarchy
Suppressing Opinion
Fascism

Violence
Suppressing Free Speech
Riots
Anarchy
Suppressing Opinion
Fascism

Violence
Suppressing Free Speech
Riots
Anarchy
Suppressing Opinion
Fascism

Violence
Suppressing Free Speech
Riots
Anarchy
Suppressing Opinion
Fascism

Violence
Suppressing Free Speech
Riots
Anarchy
Suppressing Opinion
Fascism

Violence
Suppressing Free Speech
Riots
Anarchy
Suppressing Opinion
Fascism

Violence
Suppressing Free Speech
Riots
Anarchy
Suppressing Opinion
Fascism

Violence
Suppressing Free Speech
Riots
Anarchy
Suppressing Opinion
Fascism

Violence
Suppressing Free Speech
Riots
Anarchy
Suppressing Opinion
Fascism

Violence
Suppressing Free Speech
Riots
Anarchy
Suppressing Opinion
Fascism

Violence
Suppressing Free Speech
Riots
Anarchy
Suppressing Opinion
Fascism

Violence
Suppressing Free Speech
Riots
Anarchy
Suppressing Opinion
Fascism

Violence
Suppressing Free Speech
Riots
Anarchy
Suppressing Opinion
Fascism

Violence
Suppressing Free Speech
Riots
Anarchy
Suppressing Opinion
Fascism

Violence
Suppressing Free Speech
Riots
Anarchy
Suppressing Opinion
Fascism

Violence
Suppressing Free Speech
Riots
Anarchy
Suppressing Opinion
Fascism

Violence
Suppressing Free Speech
Riots
Anarchy
Suppressing Opinion
Fascism

Violence
Suppressing Free Speech
Riots
Anarchy
Suppressing Opinion
Fascism

Violence
Suppressing Free Speech
Riots
Anarchy
Suppressing Opinion
Fascism

Violence
Suppressing Free Speech
Riots
Anarchy
Suppressing Opinion
Fascism

Violence
Suppressing Free Speech
Riots
Anarchy
Suppressing Opinion
Fascism

Violence
Suppressing Free Speech
Riots
Anarchy
Suppressing Opinion
Fascism

Violence
Suppressing Free Speech
Riots
Anarchy
Suppressing Opinion
Fascism

Violence
Suppressing Free Speech
Riots
Anarchy
Suppressing Opinion
Fascism

Violence
Suppressing Free Speech
Riots
Anarchy
Suppressing Opinion
Fascism

Violence
Suppressing Free Speech
Riots
Anarchy
Suppressing Opinion
Fascism

Violence
Suppressing Free Speech
Riots
Anarchy
Suppressing Opinion
Fascism

Violence
Suppressing Free Speech
Riots
Anarchy
Suppressing Opinion
Fascism

Violence
Suppressing Free Speech
Riots
Anarchy
Suppressing Opinion
Fascism

Violence
Suppressing Free Speech
Riots
Anarchy
Suppressing Opinion
Fascism

Violence
Suppressing Free Speech
Riots
Anarchy
Suppressing Opinion
Fascism

Violence
Suppressing Free Speech
Riots
Anarchy
Suppressing Opinion
Fascism

Violence
Suppressing Free Speech
Riots
Anarchy
Suppressing Opinion
Fascism

Violence
Suppressing Free Speech
Riots
Anarchy
Suppressing Opinion
Fascism

Violence
Suppressing Free Speech
Riots
Anarchy
Suppressing Opinion
Fascism

Violence
Suppressing Free Speech
Riots
Anarchy
Suppressing Opinion
Fascism

Violence
Suppressing Free Speech
Riots
Anarchy
Suppressing Opinion
Fascism

Violence
Suppressing Free Speech
Riots
Anarchy
Suppressing Opinion
Fascism

Violence
Suppressing Free Speech
Riots
Anarchy
Suppressing Opinion
Fascism

Violence
Suppressing Free Speech
Riots
Anarchy
Suppressing Opinion
Fascism

Violence
Suppressing Free Speech
Riots
Anarchy
Suppressing Opinion
Fascism

Violence
Suppressing Free Speech
Riots
Anarchy
Suppressing Opinion
Fascism

Violence
Suppressing Free Speech
Riots
Anarchy
Suppressing Opinion
Fascism

Violence
Suppressing Free Speech
Riots
Anarchy
Suppressing Opinion
Fascism

Violence
Suppressing Free Speech
Riots
Anarchy
Suppressing Opinion
Fascism

Violence
Suppressing Free Speech
Riots
Anarchy
Suppressing Opinion
Fascism

Violence
Suppressing Free Speech
Riots
Anarchy
Suppressing Opinion
Fascism

Violence
Suppressing Free Speech
Riots
Anarchy
Suppressing Opinion
Fascism

Violence
Suppressing Free Speech
Riots
Anarchy
Suppressing Opinion
Fascism

Violence
Suppressing Free Speech
Riots
Anarchy
Suppressing Opinion
Fascism

Violence
Suppressing Free Speech
Riots
Anarchy
Suppressing Opinion
Fascism

Violence
Suppressing Free Speech
Riots
Anarchy
Suppressing Opinion
Fascism

Violence
Suppressing Free Speech
Riots
Anarchy
Suppressing Opinion
Fascism

Violence
Suppressing Free Speech
Riots
Anarchy
Suppressing Opinion
Fascism

Violence
Suppressing Free Speech
Riots
Anarchy
Suppressing Opinion
Fascism

Violence
Suppressing Free Speech
Riots
Anarchy
Suppressing Opinion
Fascism

Violence
Suppressing Free Speech
Riots
Anarchy
Suppressing Opinion
Fascism

Violence
Suppressing Free Speech
Riots
Anarchy
Suppressing Opinion
Fascism

Violence

Suppressing Free Speech

Riots

Anarchy

Suppressing Opinion

Fascism

Violence

Suppressing Free Speech

Riots

Anarchy

Suppressing Opinion

Fascism

Violence

Suppressing Free Speech

Riots

Anarchy

Suppressing Opinion

Fascism

Violence
Suppressing Free Speech
Riots
Anarchy
Suppressing Opinion
Fascism

Violence
Suppressing Free Speech
Riots
Anarchy
Suppressing Opinion
Fascism

Violence
Suppressing Free Speech
Riots
Anarchy
Suppressing Opinion
Fascism

Violence
Suppressing Free Speech
Riots
Anarchy
Suppressing Opinion
Fascism

Violence
Suppressing Free Speech
Riots
Anarchy
Suppressing Opinion
Fascism

Violence
Suppressing Free Speech
Riots
Anarchy
Suppressing Opinion
Fascism

Violence
Suppressing Free Speech
Riots
Anarchy
Suppressing Opinion
Fascism

Violence
Suppressing Free Speech
Riots
Anarchy
Suppressing Opinion
Fascism

Violence
Suppressing Free Speech
Riots
Anarchy
Suppressing Opinion
Fascism

Violence
Suppressing Free Speech
Riots
Anarchy
Suppressing Opinion
Fascism

Violence
Suppressing Free Speech
Riots
Anarchy
Suppressing Opinion
Fascism

Violence
Suppressing Free Speech
Riots
Anarchy
Suppressing Opinion
Fascism

Violence
Suppressing Free Speech
Riots
Anarchy
Suppressing Opinion
Fascism

Violence
Suppressing Free Speech
Riots
Anarchy
Suppressing Opinion
Fascism

Violence
Suppressing Free Speech
Riots
Anarchy
Suppressing Opinion
Fascism

Violence
Suppressing Free Speech
Riots
Anarchy
Suppressing Opinion
Fascism

Violence
Suppressing Free Speech
Riots
Anarchy
Suppressing Opinion
Fascism

Violence
Suppressing Free Speech
Riots
Anarchy
Suppressing Opinion
Fascism

Violence
Suppressing Free Speech
Riots
Anarchy
Suppressing Opinion
Fascism

Violence
Suppressing Free Speech
Riots
Anarchy
Suppressing Opinion
Fascism

Violence
Suppressing Free Speech
Riots
Anarchy
Suppressing Opinion
Fascism

Violence
Suppressing Free Speech
Riots
Anarchy
Suppressing Opinion
Fascism

Violence
Suppressing Free Speech
Riots
Anarchy
Suppressing Opinion
Fascism

Violence
Suppressing Free Speech
Riots
Anarchy
Suppressing Opinion
Fascism

Violence
Suppressing Free Speech
Riots
Anarchy
Suppressing Opinion
Fascism

Violence
Suppressing Free Speech
Riots
Anarchy
Suppressing Opinion
Fascism

Violence
Suppressing Free Speech
Riots
Anarchy
Suppressing Opinion
Fascism

Violence
Suppressing Free Speech
Riots
Anarchy
Suppressing Opinion
Fascism

Violence
Suppressing Free Speech
Riots
Anarchy
Suppressing Opinion
Fascism

Violence
Suppressing Free Speech
Riots
Anarchy
Suppressing Opinion
Fascism

Violence
Suppressing Free Speech
Riots
Anarchy
Suppressing Opinion
Fascism

Violence
Suppressing Free Speech
Riots
Anarchy
Suppressing Opinion
Fascism

Violence
Suppressing Free Speech
Riots
Anarchy
Suppressing Opinion
Fascism

Violence
Suppressing Free Speech
Riots
Anarchy
Suppressing Opinion
Fascism

Violence
Suppressing Free Speech
Riots
Anarchy
Suppressing Opinion
Fascism

Violence
Suppressing Free Speech
Riots
Anarchy
Suppressing Opinion
Fascism

Violence
Suppressing Free Speech
Riots
Anarchy
Suppressing Opinion
Fascism

Violence
Suppressing Free Speech
Riots
Anarchy
Suppressing Opinion
Fascism

Violence
Suppressing Free Speech
Riots
Anarchy
Suppressing Opinion
Fascism

Violence
Suppressing Free Speech
Riots
Anarchy
Suppressing Opinion
Fascism

Violence
Suppressing Free Speech
Riots
Anarchy
Suppressing Opinion
Fascism

Violence
Suppressing Free Speech
Riots
Anarchy
Suppressing Opinion
Fascism

Violence
Suppressing Free Speech
Riots
Anarchy
Suppressing Opinion
Fascism

Violence
Suppressing Free Speech
Riots
Anarchy
Suppressing Opinion
Fascism

Violence
Suppressing Free Speech
Riots
Anarchy
Suppressing Opinion
Fascism

Violence
Suppressing Free Speech
Riots
Anarchy
Suppressing Opinion
Fascism

Violence
Suppressing Free Speech
Riots
Anarchy
Suppressing Opinion
Fascism

Violence
Suppressing Free Speech
Riots
Anarchy
Suppressing Opinion
Fascism

Violence
Suppressing Free Speech
Riots
Anarchy
Suppressing Opinion
Fascism

Violence
Suppressing Free Speech
Riots
Anarchy
Suppressing Opinion
Fascism

Violence
Suppressing Free Speech
Riots
Anarchy
Suppressing Opinion
Fascism

Violence
Suppressing Free Speech
Riots
Anarchy
Suppressing Opinion
Fascism

Violence
Suppressing Free Speech
Riots
Anarchy
Suppressing Opinion
Fascism

Violence
Suppressing Free Speech
Riots
Anarchy
Suppressing Opinion
Fascism

Violence
Suppressing Free Speech
Riots
Anarchy
Suppressing Opinion
Fascism

Violence
Suppressing Free Speech
Riots
Anarchy
Suppressing Opinion
Fascism

Violence
Suppressing Free Speech
Riots
Anarchy
Suppressing Opinion
Fascism

Violence
Suppressing Free Speech
Riots
Anarchy
Suppressing Opinion
Fascism

Violence
Suppressing Free Speech
Riots
Anarchy
Suppressing Opinion
Fascism

Violence
Suppressing Free Speech
Riots
Anarchy
Suppressing Opinion
Fascism

Violence
Suppressing Free Speech
Riots
Anarchy
Suppressing Opinion
Fascism

Violence
Suppressing Free Speech
Riots
Anarchy
Suppressing Opinion
Fascism

Violence
Suppressing Free Speech
Riots
Anarchy
Suppressing Opinion
Fascism

Violence
Suppressing Free Speech
Riots
Anarchy
Suppressing Opinion
Fascism

Violence
Suppressing Free Speech
Riots
Anarchy
Suppressing Opinion
Fascism

Violence
Suppressing Free Speech
Riots
Anarchy
Suppressing Opinion
Fascism

Violence
Suppressing Free Speech
Riots
Anarchy
Suppressing Opinion
Fascism

Violence
Suppressing Free Speech
Riots
Anarchy
Suppressing Opinion
Fascism

Violence
Suppressing Free Speech
Riots
Anarchy
Suppressing Opinion
Fascism

Violence
Suppressing Free Speech
Riots
Anarchy
Suppressing Opinion
Fascism

Violence
Suppressing Free Speech
Riots
Anarchy
Suppressing Opinion
Fascism

Violence
Suppressing Free Speech
Riots
Anarchy
Suppressing Opinion
Fascism

Violence
Suppressing Free Speech
Riots
Anarchy
Suppressing Opinion
Fascism

Violence
Suppressing Free Speech
Riots
Anarchy
Suppressing Opinion
Fascism

Violence
Suppressing Free Speech
Riots
Anarchy
Suppressing Opinion
Fascism

Violence
Suppressing Free Speech
Riots
Anarchy
Suppressing Opinion
Fascism

Violence
Suppressing Free Speech
Riots
Anarchy
Suppressing Opinion
Fascism

Violence
Suppressing Free Speech
Riots
Anarchy
Suppressing Opinion
Fascism

Violence
Suppressing Free Speech
Riots
Anarchy
Suppressing Opinion
Fascism

Violence
Suppressing Free Speech
Riots
Anarchy
Suppressing Opinion
Fascism

Violence
Suppressing Free Speech
Riots
Anarchy
Suppressing Opinion
Fascism

Violence
Suppressing Free Speech
Riots
Anarchy
Suppressing Opinion
Fascism

Violence
Suppressing Free Speech
Riots
Anarchy
Suppressing Opinion
Fascism

Violence
Suppressing Free Speech
Riots
Anarchy
Suppressing Opinion
Fascism

Violence
Suppressing Free Speech
Riots
Anarchy
Suppressing Opinion
Fascism

Violence
Suppressing Free Speech
Riots
Anarchy
Suppressing Opinion
Fascism

Violence
Suppressing Free Speech
Riots
Anarchy
Suppressing Opinion
Fascism

Violence
Suppressing Free Speech
Riots
Anarchy
Suppressing Opinion
Fascism

Violence
Suppressing Free Speech
Riots
Anarchy
Suppressing Opinion
Fascism

Violence
Suppressing Free Speech
Riots
Anarchy
Suppressing Opinion
Fascism

Violence
Suppressing Free Speech
Riots
Anarchy
Suppressing Opinion
Fascism

Violence
Suppressing Free Speech
Riots
Anarchy
Suppressing Opinion
Fascism

Violence
Suppressing Free Speech
Riots
Anarchy
Suppressing Opinion
Fascism

Violence
Suppressing Free Speech
Riots
Anarchy
Suppressing Opinion
Fascism

Violence
Suppressing Free Speech
Riots
Anarchy
Suppressing Opinion
Fascism

Violence
Suppressing Free Speech
Riots
Anarchy
Suppressing Opinion
Fascism

Violence
Suppressing Free Speech
Riots
Anarchy
Suppressing Opinion
Fascism

Violence
Suppressing Free Speech
Riots
Anarchy
Suppressing Opinion
Fascism

Violence
Suppressing Free Speech
Riots
Anarchy
Suppressing Opinion
Fascism

Violence
Suppressing Free Speech
Riots
Anarchy
Suppressing Opinion
Fascism

Violence
Suppressing Free Speech
Riots
Anarchy
Suppressing Opinion
Fascism

Violence
Suppressing Free Speech
Riots
Anarchy
Suppressing Opinion
Fascism

Violence
Suppressing Free Speech
Riots
Anarchy
Suppressing Opinion
Fascism

Violence
Suppressing Free Speech
Riots
Anarchy
Suppressing Opinion
Fascism

Violence
Suppressing Free Speech
Riots
Anarchy
Suppressing Opinion
Fascism

Violence
Suppressing Free Speech
Riots
Anarchy
Suppressing Opinion
Fascism

Violence
Suppressing Free Speech
Riots
Anarchy
Suppressing Opinion
Fascism

Violence
Suppressing Free Speech
Riots
Anarchy
Suppressing Opinion
Fascism

Violence
Suppressing Free Speech
Riots
Anarchy
Suppressing Opinion
Fascism

Violence
Suppressing Free Speech
Riots
Anarchy
Suppressing Opinion
Fascism

Violence
Suppressing Free Speech
Riots
Anarchy
Suppressing Opinion
Fascism

Violence
Suppressing Free Speech
Riots
Anarchy
Suppressing Opinion
Fascism

Violence
Suppressing Free Speech
Riots
Anarchy
Suppressing Opinion
Fascism

Violence
Suppressing Free Speech
Riots
Anarchy
Suppressing Opinion
Fascism

Violence
Suppressing Free Speech
Riots
Anarchy
Suppressing Opinion
Fascism

Violence
Suppressing Free Speech
Riots
Anarchy
Suppressing Opinion
Fascism

Violence
Suppressing Free Speech
Riots
Anarchy
Suppressing Opinion
Fascism

Violence
Suppressing Free Speech
Riots
Anarchy
Suppressing Opinion
Fascism

Violence
Suppressing Free Speech
Riots
Anarchy
Suppressing Opinion
Fascism

Violence
Suppressing Free Speech
Riots
Anarchy
Suppressing Opinion
Fascism

Violence
Suppressing Free Speech
Riots
Anarchy
Suppressing Opinion
Fascism

Violence
Suppressing Free Speech
Riots
Anarchy
Suppressing Opinion
Fascism

Violence
Suppressing Free Speech
Riots
Anarchy
Suppressing Opinion
Fascism

Violence
Suppressing Free Speech
Riots
Anarchy
Suppressing Opinion
Fascism

Violence
Suppressing Free Speech
Riots
Anarchy
Suppressing Opinion
Fascism

Violence
Suppressing Free Speech
Riots
Anarchy
Suppressing Opinion
Fascism

Violence
Suppressing Free Speech
Riots
Anarchy
Suppressing Opinion
Fascism

Violence
Suppressing Free Speech
Riots
Anarchy
Suppressing Opinion
Fascism

Violence
Suppressing Free Speech
Riots
Anarchy
Suppressing Opinion
Fascism

Violence
Suppressing Free Speech
Riots
Anarchy
Suppressing Opinion
Fascism

Violence
Suppressing Free Speech
Riots
Anarchy
Suppressing Opinion
Fascism

Violence
Suppressing Free Speech
Riots
Anarchy
Suppressing Opinion
Fascism

Violence
Suppressing Free Speech
Riots
Anarchy
Suppressing Opinion
Fascism

Violence
Suppressing Free Speech
Riots
Anarchy
Suppressing Opinion
Fascism

Violence
Suppressing Free Speech
Riots
Anarchy
Suppressing Opinion
Fascism

Violence
Suppressing Free Speech
Riots
Anarchy
Suppressing Opinion
Fascism

Violence
Suppressing Free Speech
Riots
Anarchy
Suppressing Opinion
Fascism

Violence
Suppressing Free Speech
Riots
Anarchy
Suppressing Opinion
Fascism

Violence
Suppressing Free Speech
Riots
Anarchy
Suppressing Opinion
Fascism

Violence
Suppressing Free Speech
Riots
Anarchy
Suppressing Opinion
Fascism

Violence
Suppressing Free Speech
Riots
Anarchy
Suppressing Opinion
Fascism

Violence
Suppressing Free Speech
Riots
Anarchy
Suppressing Opinion
Fascism

Violence
Suppressing Free Speech
Riots
Anarchy
Suppressing Opinion
Fascism

Violence
Suppressing Free Speech
Riots
Anarchy
Suppressing Opinion
Fascism

Violence
Suppressing Free Speech
Riots
Anarchy
Suppressing Opinion
Fascism

Violence
Suppressing Free Speech
Riots
Anarchy
Suppressing Opinion
Fascism

Violence
Suppressing Free Speech
Riots
Anarchy
Suppressing Opinion
Fascism

Violence
Suppressing Free Speech
Riots
Anarchy
Suppressing Opinion
Fascism

Violence
Suppressing Free Speech
Riots
Anarchy
Suppressing Opinion
Fascism

Violence
Suppressing Free Speech
Riots
Anarchy
Suppressing Opinion
Fascism

Violence
Suppressing Free Speech
Riots
Anarchy
Suppressing Opinion
Fascism

Violence
Suppressing Free Speech
Riots
Anarchy
Suppressing Opinion
Fascism

Violence
Suppressing Free Speech
Riots
Anarchy
Suppressing Opinion
Fascism

Violence
Suppressing Free Speech
Riots
Anarchy
Suppressing Opinion
Fascism

Violence
Suppressing Free Speech
Riots
Anarchy
Suppressing Opinion
Fascism

Violence
Suppressing Free Speech
Riots
Anarchy
Suppressing Opinion
Fascism

Violence
Suppressing Free Speech
Riots
Anarchy
Suppressing Opinion
Fascism

Violence
Suppressing Free Speech
Riots
Anarchy
Suppressing Opinion
Fascism

Violence
Suppressing Free Speech
Riots
Anarchy
Suppressing Opinion
Fascism

Violence
Suppressing Free Speech
Riots
Anarchy
Suppressing Opinion
Fascism

Violence
Suppressing Free Speech
Riots
Anarchy
Suppressing Opinion
Fascism

Violence
Suppressing Free Speech
Riots
Anarchy
Suppressing Opinion
Fascism

Violence
Suppressing Free Speech
Riots
Anarchy
Suppressing Opinion
Fascism

Violence
Suppressing Free Speech
Riots
Anarchy
Suppressing Opinion
Fascism

Violence
Suppressing Free Speech
Riots
Anarchy
Suppressing Opinion
Fascism

Violence
Suppressing Free Speech
Riots
Anarchy
Suppressing Opinion
Fascism

Violence
Suppressing Free Speech
Riots
Anarchy
Suppressing Opinion
Fascism

Violence
Suppressing Free Speech
Riots
Anarchy
Suppressing Opinion
Fascism

Violence
Suppressing Free Speech
Riots
Anarchy
Suppressing Opinion
Fascism

Violence
Suppressing Free Speech
Riots
Anarchy
Suppressing Opinion
Fascism

Violence
Suppressing Free Speech
Riots
Anarchy
Suppressing Opinion
Fascism

Violence
Suppressing Free Speech
Riots
Anarchy
Suppressing Opinion
Fascism

Violence
Suppressing Free Speech
Riots
Anarchy
Suppressing Opinion
Fascism

Violence
Suppressing Free Speech
Riots
Anarchy
Suppressing Opinion
Fascism

Violence
Suppressing Free Speech
Riots
Anarchy
Suppressing Opinion
Fascism

Violence
Suppressing Free Speech
Riots
Anarchy
Suppressing Opinion
Fascism

Violence
Suppressing Free Speech
Riots
Anarchy
Suppressing Opinion
Fascism

Violence
Suppressing Free Speech
Riots
Anarchy
Suppressing Opinion
Fascism

Violence
Suppressing Free Speech
Riots
Anarchy
Suppressing Opinion
Fascism

Violence
Suppressing Free Speech
Riots
Anarchy
Suppressing Opinion
Fascism

Violence
Suppressing Free Speech
Riots
Anarchy
Suppressing Opinion
Fascism

Violence
Suppressing Free Speech
Riots
Anarchy
Suppressing Opinion
Fascism

Violence
Suppressing Free Speech
Riots
Anarchy
Suppressing Opinion
Fascism

Violence
Suppressing Free Speech
Riots
Anarchy
Suppressing Opinion
Fascism

Violence
Suppressing Free Speech
Riots
Anarchy
Suppressing Opinion
Fascism

Violence
Suppressing Free Speech
Riots
Anarchy
Suppressing Opinion
Fascism

Violence
Suppressing Free Speech
Riots
Anarchy
Suppressing Opinion
Fascism

Violence
Suppressing Free Speech
Riots
Anarchy
Suppressing Opinion
Fascism

Violence
Suppressing Free Speech
Riots
Anarchy
Suppressing Opinion
Fascism

Violence
Suppressing Free Speech
Riots
Anarchy
Suppressing Opinion
Fascism

Violence
Suppressing Free Speech
Riots
Anarchy
Suppressing Opinion
Fascism

Violence
Suppressing Free Speech
Riots
Anarchy
Suppressing Opinion
Fascism

Violence

Suppressing Free Speech

Riots

Anarchy

Suppressing Opinion

Fascism

Violence

Suppressing Free Speech

Riots

Anarchy

Suppressing Opinion

Fascism

Violence

Suppressing Free Speech

Riots

Anarchy

Suppressing Opinion

Fascism

Violence
Suppressing Free Speech
Riots
Anarchy
Suppressing Opinion
Fascism

Violence
Suppressing Free Speech
Riots
Anarchy
Suppressing Opinion
Fascism

Violence
Suppressing Free Speech
Riots
Anarchy
Suppressing Opinion
Fascism

Violence
Suppressing Free Speech
Riots
Anarchy
Suppressing Opinion
Fascism

Violence
Suppressing Free Speech
Riots
Anarchy
Suppressing Opinion
Fascism

Violence
Suppressing Free Speech
Riots
Anarchy
Suppressing Opinion
Fascism

Violence
Suppressing Free Speech
Riots
Anarchy
Suppressing Opinion
Fascism

Violence
Suppressing Free Speech
Riots
Anarchy
Suppressing Opinion
Fascism

Violence
Suppressing Free Speech
Riots
Anarchy
Suppressing Opinion
Fascism

Violence
Suppressing Free Speech
Riots
Anarchy
Suppressing Opinion
Fascism

Violence
Suppressing Free Speech
Riots
Anarchy
Suppressing Opinion
Fascism

Violence
Suppressing Free Speech
Riots
Anarchy
Suppressing Opinion
Fascism

Violence
Suppressing Free Speech
Riots
Anarchy
Suppressing Opinion
Fascism

Violence
Suppressing Free Speech
Riots
Anarchy
Suppressing Opinion
Fascism

Violence
Suppressing Free Speech
Riots
Anarchy
Suppressing Opinion
Fascism

Violence
Suppressing Free Speech
Riots
Anarchy
Suppressing Opinion
Fascism

Violence
Suppressing Free Speech
Riots
Anarchy
Suppressing Opinion
Fascism

Violence
Suppressing Free Speech
Riots
Anarchy
Suppressing Opinion
Fascism

Violence
Suppressing Free Speech
Riots
Anarchy
Suppressing Opinion
Fascism

Violence
Suppressing Free Speech
Riots
Anarchy
Suppressing Opinion
Fascism

Violence
Suppressing Free Speech
Riots
Anarchy
Suppressing Opinion
Fascism

Violence
Suppressing Free Speech
Riots
Anarchy
Suppressing Opinion
Fascism

Violence
Suppressing Free Speech
Riots
Anarchy
Suppressing Opinion
Fascism

Violence
Suppressing Free Speech
Riots
Anarchy
Suppressing Opinion
Fascism

Violence
Suppressing Free Speech
Riots
Anarchy
Suppressing Opinion
Fascism

Violence
Suppressing Free Speech
Riots
Anarchy
Suppressing Opinion
Fascism

Violence
Suppressing Free Speech
Riots
Anarchy
Suppressing Opinion
Fascism

Violence
Suppressing Free Speech
Riots
Anarchy
Suppressing Opinion
Fascism

Violence
Suppressing Free Speech
Riots
Anarchy
Suppressing Opinion
Fascism

Violence
Suppressing Free Speech
Riots
Anarchy
Suppressing Opinion
Fascism

Violence
Suppressing Free Speech
Riots
Anarchy
Suppressing Opinion
Fascism

Violence
Suppressing Free Speech
Riots
Anarchy
Suppressing Opinion
Fascism

Violence
Suppressing Free Speech
Riots
Anarchy
Suppressing Opinion
Fascism

Violence
Suppressing Free Speech
Riots
Anarchy
Suppressing Opinion
Fascism

Violence
Suppressing Free Speech
Riots
Anarchy
Suppressing Opinion
Fascism

Violence
Suppressing Free Speech
Riots
Anarchy
Suppressing Opinion
Fascism

Violence
Suppressing Free Speech
Riots
Anarchy
Suppressing Opinion
Fascism

Violence
Suppressing Free Speech
Riots
Anarchy
Suppressing Opinion
Fascism

Violence
Suppressing Free Speech
Riots
Anarchy
Suppressing Opinion
Fascism

Violence
Suppressing Free Speech
Riots
Anarchy
Suppressing Opinion
Fascism

Violence
Suppressing Free Speech
Riots
Anarchy
Suppressing Opinion
Fascism

Violence
Suppressing Free Speech
Riots
Anarchy
Suppressing Opinion
Fascism

Violence
Suppressing Free Speech
Riots
Anarchy
Suppressing Opinion
Fascism

Violence
Suppressing Free Speech
Riots
Anarchy
Suppressing Opinion
Fascism

Violence
Suppressing Free Speech
Riots
Anarchy
Suppressing Opinion
Fascism

Violence
Suppressing Free Speech
Riots
Anarchy
Suppressing Opinion
Fascism

Violence
Suppressing Free Speech
Riots
Anarchy
Suppressing Opinion
Fascism

Violence
Suppressing Free Speech
Riots
Anarchy
Suppressing Opinion
Fascism

Violence
Suppressing Free Speech
Riots
Anarchy
Suppressing Opinion
Fascism

Violence
Suppressing Free Speech
Riots
Anarchy
Suppressing Opinion
Fascism

Violence
Suppressing Free Speech
Riots
Anarchy
Suppressing Opinion
Fascism

Violence
Suppressing Free Speech
Riots
Anarchy
Suppressing Opinion
Fascism

Violence
Suppressing Free Speech
Riots
Anarchy
Suppressing Opinion
Fascism

Violence
Suppressing Free Speech
Riots
Anarchy
Suppressing Opinion
Fascism

Violence
Suppressing Free Speech
Riots
Anarchy
Suppressing Opinion
Fascism

Violence
Suppressing Free Speech
Riots
Anarchy
Suppressing Opinion
Fascism

Violence
Suppressing Free Speech
Riots
Anarchy
Suppressing Opinion
Fascism

Violence
Suppressing Free Speech
Riots
Anarchy
Suppressing Opinion
Fascism

Violence
Suppressing Free Speech
Riots
Anarchy
Suppressing Opinion
Fascism

Violence
Suppressing Free Speech
Riots
Anarchy
Suppressing Opinion
Fascism

Violence
Suppressing Free Speech
Riots
Anarchy
Suppressing Opinion
Fascism

Violence
Suppressing Free Speech
Riots
Anarchy
Suppressing Opinion
Fascism

Violence
Suppressing Free Speech
Riots
Anarchy
Suppressing Opinion
Fascism

Violence
Suppressing Free Speech
Riots
Anarchy
Suppressing Opinion
Fascism

Violence
Suppressing Free Speech
Riots
Anarchy
Suppressing Opinion
Fascism

Violence
Suppressing Free Speech
Riots
Anarchy
Suppressing Opinion
Fascism

Violence
Suppressing Free Speech
Riots
Anarchy
Suppressing Opinion
Fascism

Violence
Suppressing Free Speech
Riots
Anarchy
Suppressing Opinion
Fascism

Violence
Suppressing Free Speech
Riots
Anarchy
Suppressing Opinion
Fascism

Violence
Suppressing Free Speech
Riots
Anarchy
Suppressing Opinion
Fascism

Violence
Suppressing Free Speech
Riots
Anarchy
Suppressing Opinion
Fascism

Violence
Suppressing Free Speech
Riots
Anarchy
Suppressing Opinion
Fascism

Violence
Suppressing Free Speech
Riots
Anarchy
Suppressing Opinion
Fascism

Violence
Suppressing Free Speech
Riots
Anarchy
Suppressing Opinion
Fascism

Violence
Suppressing Free Speech
Riots
Anarchy
Suppressing Opinion
Fascism

Violence
Suppressing Free Speech
Riots
Anarchy
Suppressing Opinion
Fascism

Violence
Suppressing Free Speech
Riots
Anarchy
Suppressing Opinion
Fascism

Violence
Suppressing Free Speech
Riots
Anarchy
Suppressing Opinion
Fascism

Violence
Suppressing Free Speech
Riots
Anarchy
Suppressing Opinion
Fascism

Violence
Suppressing Free Speech
Riots
Anarchy
Suppressing Opinion
Fascism

Violence
Suppressing Free Speech
Riots
Anarchy
Suppressing Opinion
Fascism

Violence
Suppressing Free Speech
Riots
Anarchy
Suppressing Opinion
Fascism

Violence
Suppressing Free Speech
Riots
Anarchy
Suppressing Opinion
Fascism

Violence
Suppressing Free Speech
Riots
Anarchy
Suppressing Opinion
Fascism

Violence
Suppressing Free Speech
Riots
Anarchy
Suppressing Opinion
Fascism

Violence
Suppressing Free Speech
Riots
Anarchy
Suppressing Opinion
Fascism

Violence
Suppressing Free Speech
Riots
Anarchy
Suppressing Opinion
Fascism

Violence
Suppressing Free Speech
Riots
Anarchy
Suppressing Opinion
Fascism

Violence
Suppressing Free Speech
Riots
Anarchy
Suppressing Opinion
Fascism

Violence
Suppressing Free Speech
Riots
Anarchy
Suppressing Opinion
Fascism

Violence

Suppressing Free Speech

Riots

Anarchy

Suppressing Opinion

Fascism

Violence

Suppressing Free Speech

Riots

Anarchy

Suppressing Opinion

Fascism

Violence

Suppressing Free Speech

Riots

Anarchy

Suppressing Opinion

Fascism

Violence
Suppressing Free Speech
Riots
Anarchy
Suppressing Opinion
Fascism

Violence
Suppressing Free Speech
Riots
Anarchy
Suppressing Opinion
Fascism

Violence
Suppressing Free Speech
Riots
Anarchy
Suppressing Opinion
Fascism

Violence
Suppressing Free Speech
Riots
Anarchy
Suppressing Opinion
Fascism

Violence
Suppressing Free Speech
Riots
Anarchy
Suppressing Opinion
Fascism

Violence
Suppressing Free Speech
Riots
Anarchy
Suppressing Opinion
Fascism

Violence

Suppressing Free Speech

Riots

Anarchy

Suppressing Opinion

Fascism

Violence

Suppressing Free Speech

Riots

Anarchy

Suppressing Opinion

Fascism

Violence

Suppressing Free Speech

Riots

Anarchy

Suppressing Opinion

Fascism

Violence

Suppressing Free Speech

Riots

Anarchy

Suppressing Opinion

Fascism

Violence

Suppressing Free Speech

Riots

Anarchy

Suppressing Opinion

Fascism

Violence

Suppressing Free Speech

Riots

Anarchy

Suppressing Opinion

Fascism

Violence
Suppressing Free Speech
Riots
Anarchy
Suppressing Opinion
Fascism

Violence
Suppressing Free Speech
Riots
Anarchy
Suppressing Opinion
Fascism

Violence
Suppressing Free Speech
Riots
Anarchy
Suppressing Opinion
Fascism

Violence
Suppressing Free Speech
Riots
Anarchy
Suppressing Opinion
Fascism

Violence
Suppressing Free Speech
Riots
Anarchy
Suppressing Opinion
Fascism

Violence
Suppressing Free Speech
Riots
Anarchy
Suppressing Opinion
Fascism

Violence
Suppressing Free Speech
Riots
Anarchy
Suppressing Opinion
Fascism

Violence
Suppressing Free Speech
Riots
Anarchy
Suppressing Opinion
Fascism

Violence
Suppressing Free Speech
Riots
Anarchy
Suppressing Opinion
Fascism

Violence
Suppressing Free Speech
Riots
Anarchy
Suppressing Opinion
Fascism

Violence
Suppressing Free Speech
Riots
Anarchy
Suppressing Opinion
Fascism

Violence
Suppressing Free Speech
Riots
Anarchy
Suppressing Opinion
Fascism

Violence
Suppressing Free Speech
Riots
Anarchy
Suppressing Opinion
Fascism

Violence
Suppressing Free Speech
Riots
Anarchy
Suppressing Opinion
Fascism

Violence
Suppressing Free Speech
Riots
Anarchy
Suppressing Opinion
Fascism

Violence
Suppressing Free Speech
Riots
Anarchy
Suppressing Opinion
Fascism

Violence
Suppressing Free Speech
Riots
Anarchy
Suppressing Opinion
Fascism

Violence
Suppressing Free Speech
Riots
Anarchy
Suppressing Opinion
Fascism

Violence
Suppressing Free Speech
Riots
Anarchy
Suppressing Opinion
Fascism

Violence
Suppressing Free Speech
Riots
Anarchy
Suppressing Opinion
Fascism

Violence
Suppressing Free Speech
Riots
Anarchy
Suppressing Opinion
Fascism

Violence
Suppressing Free Speech
Riots
Anarchy
Suppressing Opinion
Fascism

Violence
Suppressing Free Speech
Riots
Anarchy
Suppressing Opinion
Fascism

Violence
Suppressing Free Speech
Riots
Anarchy
Suppressing Opinion
Fascism

Violence
Suppressing Free Speech
Riots
Anarchy
Suppressing Opinion
Fascism

Violence
Suppressing Free Speech
Riots
Anarchy
Suppressing Opinion
Fascism

Violence
Suppressing Free Speech
Riots
Anarchy
Suppressing Opinion
Fascism

Violence
Suppressing Free Speech
Riots
Anarchy
Suppressing Opinion
Fascism

Violence
Suppressing Free Speech
Riots
Anarchy
Suppressing Opinion
Fascism

Violence
Suppressing Free Speech
Riots
Anarchy
Suppressing Opinion
Fascism

Violence
Suppressing Free Speech
Riots
Anarchy
Suppressing Opinion
Fascism

Violence
Suppressing Free Speech
Riots
Anarchy
Suppressing Opinion
Fascism

Violence
Suppressing Free Speech
Riots
Anarchy
Suppressing Opinion
Fascism

Violence
Suppressing Free Speech
Riots
Anarchy
Suppressing Opinion
Fascism

Violence
Suppressing Free Speech
Riots
Anarchy
Suppressing Opinion
Fascism

Violence
Suppressing Free Speech
Riots
Anarchy
Suppressing Opinion
Fascism

Violence
Suppressing Free Speech
Riots
Anarchy
Suppressing Opinion
Fascism

Violence
Suppressing Free Speech
Riots
Anarchy
Suppressing Opinion
Fascism

Violence
Suppressing Free Speech
Riots
Anarchy
Suppressing Opinion
Fascism

Violence
Suppressing Free Speech
Riots
Anarchy
Suppressing Opinion
Fascism

Violence
Suppressing Free Speech
Riots
Anarchy
Suppressing Opinion
Fascism

Violence
Suppressing Free Speech
Riots
Anarchy
Suppressing Opinion
Fascism

Violence
Suppressing Free Speech
Riots
Anarchy
Suppressing Opinion
Fascism

Violence
Suppressing Free Speech
Riots
Anarchy
Suppressing Opinion
Fascism

Violence
Suppressing Free Speech
Riots
Anarchy
Suppressing Opinion
Fascism

Violence
Suppressing Free Speech
Riots
Anarchy
Suppressing Opinion
Fascism

Violence
Suppressing Free Speech
Riots
Anarchy
Suppressing Opinion
Fascism

Violence
Suppressing Free Speech
Riots
Anarchy
Suppressing Opinion
Fascism

Violence
Suppressing Free Speech
Riots
Anarchy
Suppressing Opinion
Fascism

Violence
Suppressing Free Speech
Riots
Anarchy
Suppressing Opinion
Fascism

Violence
Suppressing Free Speech
Riots
Anarchy
Suppressing Opinion
Fascism

9 781720 267584